WIN THE DAY
CHARITY

WIN THE DAY
CHARITY
WIN THE DAY
CHARITY
WIN THE DAY
CHARITY
WIN THE DAY
CHARITY
WIN THE DAY
CHARITY
WIN THE DAY
CHARITY
WIN THE DAY
CHARITY
WIN THE DAY
CHARITY
WIN THE DAY
CHARITY
WIN THE DAY
CHARITY
WIN THE DAY
CHARITY
WIN THE DAY
CHARITY
WIN THE DAY
CHARITY
WIN THE DAY
CHARITY
WIN THE DAY
CHARITY
WIN THE DAY
CHARITY
WIN THE DAY
CHARITY
WIN THE DAY
CHARITY
WIN THE DAY
CHARITY
WIN THE DAY
CHARITY
WIN THE DAY
CHARITY
WIN THE DAY
CHARITY
WIN THE DAY
CHARITY

For dear Ka'ili – The inspiration behind this book and the bravest little girl I know. Even though I was your teacher, I feel like you taught me more than I could ever teach you. I am honoured to have been part of your journey. – M.R

And, to her brave and beautiful Mum, Kristy. I am in constant awe of your strength. You are an absolute inspiration, and your passion and positivity will forever amaze me. I love you dearly. – M.R

For Mabel and Esme. The two halves of my heart x – J.B

A portion from every book sale will be donated to the 'Win the Day' Charity.

First Published in August, 2023.

Text copyright © Meg Rees 2023

Illustrations copyright © Jessica Blair 2023

ISBN 978-0-6458996-0-3 (hardcopy)

ISBN 978-0-6458996-1-0 (paperback)

WIN THE DAY
CHARITY

https://www.wintheday.org.au

When someone you love is sick

Written by Meg Rees

Illustrated by Jessica Blair

When someone you love is sick,

you might be shocked to hear

that the very person that is sick,

is someone you love so dear.

When someone you love is sick,
they might feel a lot of pain.
They will need to go to a doctor
so that they can help explain.

When someone you love is sick,
they need family and friend support.
Sometimes your loved one's doctor,
might have to give a bad report.

When someone you love is sick,
they might have to leave their home.
They need your constant love and support
so they don't feel all alone.

When someone you love is sick,

they leave family and friends behind.

They'll have treatment at the hospital,

so be sure to keep them in mind.

ONCOLOGY

ROOMS
197 – 201

EMERGENCY

When someone you love is sick,
they might miss important things.
Birthdays, Weddings, Christmas, Easter
and all the happy times they bring.

When someone you love is sick,

the doctor will do some tests.

Through this time your loved one

may experience some side effects.

When someone you love is sick,
they might lose all their hair.
They may wear hats and beanies
so that their head is not bare.

When someone you love is sick,

there is no trick or magic cure.

The pain that comes with sickness

is a lot for someone to endure.

When someone you love is sick,
it can make you feel quite down.
It's important to stay positive
when your loved one is around.

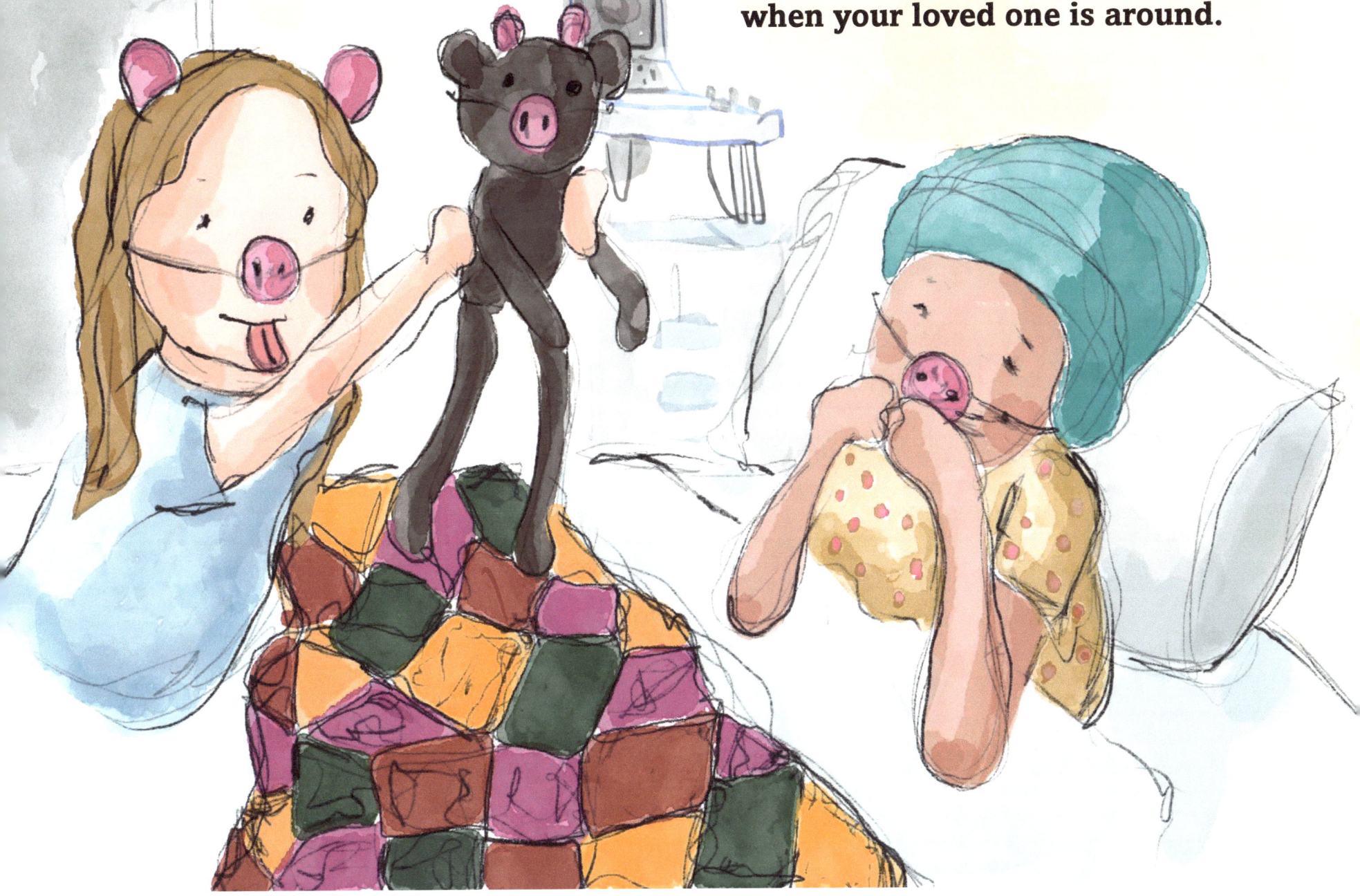

When someone you love is sick,

their carers will feel down too.

They have to be so strong and brave

to help your loved one through.

When someone you love is sick
and you don't know what to do,
it's always nice to cheer them up
when they're feeling blue.

When someone you love is sick,

you can help make them smile.

Post presents, write letters or Facetime,

even visit them once in a while.

When someone you love is sick,

it will not be an easy road.

There are some things you can do,

that will help ease the load.

When someone you love is sick,
donating to charity is one thing you can do.
If you help raise money and awareness,
it will help your loved one too.

When someone you love is sick,

it can make you feel quite sad.

Think of all your special memories,

and you're sure to feel glad.

John Dorros

spring o.

PETTING ZOO

BFFU

When someone you love is sick,

they remain hopeful to feel well.

They look forward to the day

they will ring the oncology bell.

When someone you love is sick,

remember things will be okay.

The one thing you should aim to do

is 'win every single day'.

9 780645 899603